The
Pastor-Deacon
Dynamic

By
Rev. R. L. White Jr.

Edited by Victor Singletary

R.H.Boyd
Publishing CORPORATION
A GLOBAL NAME IN PUBLISHING FOR OVER 100 YEARS

Nashville, Tennessee 37209

The
Pastor-Deacon
Dynamic

BY
REV. R. L. WHITE JR.
(Edited by Dr. Victor Singletary)

The Pastor-Deacon Dilemma
Copyright © 2003 by the R. H. Boyd Publishing Corporation
6717 Centennial Blvd.
Nashville, TN 37209-1000
ISBN 1-56742-005-2

This book was previously published as the *Preacher-Deacon Dilemma*.

All Scripture quotations are taken from the Holy Bible, *King James Version*.

Printed in the United States of America

TABLE OF CONTENTS

Addendum

DEDICATION

In appreciation to my wife Lorraine for being an inexplicable part of my life and ministry, the Mount Ephraim Baptist Church and its members for affording me the pleasure of being their pastor, Mrs. Sandra Wall for her diligence and faithfulness in typing this manuscript, and everyone who had a part in helping to bring this book to fruition. The glory belongs to God!

R. L. White

PREFACE

There is a war that goes on continuously around us, and although the average church member knows of the turmoil, it seems that no one has actually been able to quiet this silent war between the pastor and the deacons. What is all the fighting about? Many don't want to face the real issue—who is supposed to run the church, the preacher or the deacons?

From the deacons' standpoint, more times than not, the preacher is viewed not as one of the team, but as a "hired hand," one they need to watch and police because they have to protect the church from the preacher.

From the preacher's standpoint, the deacons are unnecessary evils who are "thorns in the flesh" to most pastors. Most pastors say, "I wish I didn't have deacons; the church would be better off." Many times ministers then feel that they need to assert their authority as pastor.

Over the years, this problem has put the peace of the church in jeopardy in many cities and towns. Families and churches split and acts of violence occur because preachers and deacons struggle for control.

I firmly believe preachers and deacons commit a grave injustice when they become noncommunicative, combative, and bitter. The faith of many members has been destroyed by this animosity. Some Christians may never heal from their pain. Droves of church members have left permanently damaged. They may never embrace Christianity again.

The Bible certainly does not evade the issue of conflicts. The Bible reports the conflicts as they took place. The conflict between Paul and Barnabas demonstrates that the close relationship with God did not remove conflict. The argument between Paul and Barnabas became so heated that they split over whether to take John Mark on their second missionary journey. John Mark had left them on the first mission. Paul was content that John Mark would leave them again, but Barnabas was determined to take John Mark. The Bible reports, "Barnabas took Mark, and sailed unto Cyprus; and Paul chose Silas and went through Syria and Cilicia, confirming the churches" (Acts 15:36-41). When children of God are truly saved, the love that Jesus commands that we have determines our behavior.

As preachers and deacons, we must re-examine the message we send the world due to many pastor-deacon conflicts.

Rev. R. L. White Jr.

ABOUT THE AUTHOR

The Reverend Dr. R. L. White Jr. is the son and grandson of Baptist preachers. Reared in Macon, Georgia, he graduated from Ballard Hudson High School. Later, he moved to Washington, D.C.

While in Washington, he became a deacon at Central Union Baptist Church. He preached his trial sermon on March 31, 1968, his birthday. Subsequently, he entered the Washington Baptist Seminary.

Then he organized the Mount Siloam Baptist Church of Washington, D.C., which is now pastored by one of his sons in the ministry. In late 1969, White returned to his home state of Georgia and organized the Mount Ephraim Baptist Church on June 15, 1970. On that day, a group of 13 people met and Deacon Robert Owens led an inspiring devotion. White preached a sermon and afterward, on faith alone, established Mount Ephraim with $15. Growth led to the present location, valued at $2.7 million, and membership has grown to more than 7,000 congregants.

White did not forsake his academic pursuits. He has obtained an associate of science degree at Atlanta College and a bachelor of ministry degree from Luther Rice Seminary. In 1987, he earned a master of divinity degree from the Morehouse School of Religion. During his studies, he distinguished himself by receiving the following awards:

- NAACP Religion Excellence Award (1986)
- Pastoring the Fastest Growing Church in North America (1988)
- Concerned Black Clergy Religion Award (1991)
- Who's Who Among Intellectuals in the World (1991)

White is a self-taught musician and his passion for music emerges in choral direction: Senior Choir, Recording Choir, and Mass Choir (400 voices). He has produced several albums and is the author of four books: *Baptist Beware*, *Read It Right*, and *The Pastor-Deacon Dilemma*, and *It Hurts*.

White is married to the former Lorraine Jacques. They have five children and three grandchildren. White travels extensively to numerous cities around the world conducting revivals and religious meetings. White possesses tireless energy as it relates to building God's kingdom.

Pennye Rogers
Faith Records, Inc.
Atlanta, Georgia

FOREWORD

Publisher's Note: This is the original foreword material published in the Preacher-Deacon Dilemma.

In an era of increased hostility and polarization over many issues, we need better communication techniques to civilize our discussions. This book addresses historically divisive concerns between the two servant groups in the church hierarchy.

The Greek word "diakonos" (servant) reflects the servanthood concept that preachers and deacons should model. The debates over power and control have clouded decision making in the church. A harmonious relationship among servant leaders could not exist. Yet these "official positions" must coexist within a hostile environment. Consequently, the Church suffers immensely. "Who's in charge?" is the never-ending question.

It is encouraging to share in an instrument of instruction for resolution to this dilemma. Chapter 8, "Rules of Order," contains strategies for handling conflict and achieving resolutions. More practically, the author suggests the antidote of open communication.

The Rev. R.L. White is eminently capable to address the pastor-deacon dynamic. He has the credentials of a "PK," having been birthed and reared in the home of a pastor and having pastored for many years himself.

This book contains the advice and wisdom of a clergyman who served as the first and only pastor of Mount Ephraim Baptist Church in Atlanta, Georgia, for 20 years. *Church Growth Today*, by John Vaughn, sites Mount Ephraim as one of the fastest-growing churches in North America. The citation observes the remarkable growth from the charter membership of 13 persons who met in a home to the current membership of more than 7,000 people.

Twenty years of debate and continual dialogue over authority and administrative concerns suggest the strength of this author's perspective. In this informative and candid discussion, the reader will find an appeal for solidarity befitting servant leaders of the Church instituted by the Lord Jesus Christ.

This book, along with *Baptist Beware* and *Read It Right*, is another presentation of the heart of a loving pastor. I wholeheartedly recommend this work to you.

The Rev. Hezekiah Benton Jr.
Administrative Dean, Morehouse School of Religion
Interdenominational Theological Center
Atlanta, Georgia

WHERE DID IT ALL START?

Very few people embroiled in a controversy stop to examine the origins of their views and behavior. They act upon ideas and tactics that they were taught by cultural transmission. Therefore, one should evaluate the past practices of relatives to find the beginnings of the modern-day pastor-deacon dynamics.

Where did it all start? What do I mean by "cultural transmission"? The term, most familiar to sociologists, explains the beliefs and values that pass from generation to generation. It implies that one's environment greatly impacts who one becomes and what one believes.

Many times, one ceases to question the way of life of one's upbringing. One simply acts out of the "normal actions" of those surroundings. For example, public housing began as a temporary residence until the people could afford their own housing. Time has shown that it just doesn't work that way. Many public housing tenants are now third and fourth generation tenants. Children who grow up in public housing uncritically accept this way of life as the way to live. I do not intend to stigmatize these children. I merely use public housing to demonstrate that we are a product of our environment.

Sociologists often confront the question, "How do we reverse cultural transmission?" How does cultural transmission play a part in pastor-deacon dynamics? Surprisingly, many church and worship experiences have been transmitted culturally. Often these practices have no theological significance. As an example, why do some congregations place a sheet over the Communion table? In the sight of some, Communion could not be properly celebrated without the sheet. The chair of the board or some other deacon holds up the sheet while the pastor prepares the Communion. At the beginning of the last century, there was the problem with flies. Flies have ceased to be a problem, but we still use the sheet. Why? Quite simply, we grew up using it. We accept it as the "right" way, and we unquestionably continue the practice. Many people have no idea why we do this. This is a prime example of how cultural transmission works in the church.

Shortly after slavery, as many black congregations began to grow, there was a severe shortage of good preachers. This period produced the circuit-riding preacher. In order to serve as many communities as possible, some preachers would pastor four churches, going to one each Sunday. Still today, some "once-a-month" churches exist. Others will tell you even now, "First Sunday or third Sunday is my worshiping Sunday." During this era, pastors lived a long distance from the churches they served, so the deacons handled any problems that arose during the month.

When the preacher came, church conferences on Friday and Saturday dealt with difficult issues. The usual reply from the preacher to the deacons, "Y'all fix it, and whatever you do is all right with me." Eventually, the deacons began to feel that it was their job to run the church. The preacher's job simply was to preach. The preacher essentially became a hired hand. Once this image became an accepted fact by the membership, the office of deacon assumed more power. Add that to the fact that the average church member doesn't realize that each member has a legitimate vote in church decision making. The deacons, in effect, control the church. Over several generations, this solidified as the common practice of the Baptist church.

In later years, the number of ministers increased. Increasingly educated, ministers desire to fulfill a role of pastor in many other ways than just preaching. As the preacher demands a role in the administration of church affairs, the deacons feel that the preacher trespasses on their "turf." Deacons have resisted the changes that the more "modern" preachers attempt to institute. The result is an unholy war between the preacher and deacons. At the root of the problem is the question of authority. The preacher firmly believes that the power lies in the hands of the pastor. The deacons certainly insist that they hold the power. "Authority" fights have been the downfall of many churches. Who loses? Everybody does!

Negative Beginnings
Can Be Destructive to
Future Relationships

First impressions usually are lasting impressions. Many times, the pastor-deacon relationship starts negatively because of preconceived notions about the roles of preachers or deacons. Sometimes a stigma follows a certain preacher or board of deacons. Yet the best possible relationship can only exist when there is mutual trust, love, and friendship between the preacher and deacons.

Many times, those who are responsible for the call of ministers unconsciously feel that the ministers should be beholden to them. Each time the pastor disappoints one of these people, they consider it a personal affront and hold it against the pastor. In time their disillusionment makes foes rather than friends of them. An increasing hostility toward the minister emerges, and these new foes become openly oppositional to whatever the pastor proposes to either the board or the church. This opposition raises an apprehension within ministers, causing them to distance themselves from former allies.

Preconceived notions are especially damaging when they arise from faulty facts. Occasionally deacons accept the rumors they heard about the preacher their church just called. The report given about the minister depends on the character of the person offering an impression. If the consulted person gives a particular minister a bad name, a certain board member may vote against the minister becoming a pastor. Yet if the minister is elected over that member's objections, the board member usually does not discard preconceived notions. Instead, the board member becomes a natural enemy even before the ministers are given a fair chance to prove themselves. In too many cases, if this is the first impression, it will be very hard for any minister to overcome these preconceived notions.

By the same token, there are some deacon boards that have a bad reputation, deserved or not. The word gets out that they are a hard bunch to deal with and they treat their pastor awfully. When ministers are called to the church, if these notions are a part of their expectations, they start out negatively, anticipating problems. They may not give the board a fair chance to prove that the reputation is just. The ministers treat them as if everything they have heard is true.

It is tragic that children of God allow others to determine their feelings about somebody else. Many times we have heard so much about a certain individual or group that we believe it without question. Tragically, we close our minds to certain individuals and people. With closed minds we cannot be reasonably objective in any dealings with the persons about whom we have formed preconceived notions.

What is the solution? How can the preacher and the deacons begin to build a cooperative relationship? Children of God must resist judging people before they personally know them.

"You Are Going to Accept Me, Or Else!"

The fact that preachers are carrying out God's work does not exempt them from the same emotions as other human beings. One major emotion is rejection. Perhaps we find a connection between rejection and pastor-deacon conflicts. Moreover, the psychological make-up of preachers and deacons determines their working relationship.

Unquestionably, rejection is one of the most painful emotions. When a person feels rejected, he or she thinks, "I'm not wanted; they really can do as good, or better, without me." In Abraham Maslow's Hierarchy of Human Needs, the third level of human needs is the necessity for love and belonging. Otherwise, one becomes insecure and depressed. Death is an extreme reaction to rejection. Often one tries to compensate for unmet needs. However, nothing replaces the security of belonging. Potiphar's wife showed signs of rejection (Gen. 39:7-23). She reacted violently toward Joseph after her expressed sexual interest in him and his refusal of her advances. She told her husband Potiphar that Joseph tried to rape her. Joseph was imprisoned. Why did she lie? The pain of rejection. Some people seek revenge when their unmet needs are denied.

Experience has taught me the danger of harshly rejecting someone. Several years ago, I counseled a female member of our congregation about domestic problems. I recall saying, "You must decide what you ultimately will do." I forgot about the counseling session until approximately two years later. She then called and said, "I've made up my mind." I was puzzled momentarily. "About what?" I asked. "About leaving my husband. I'm going to leave him for you," she said. Because I was stunned, I screamed, "No, you won't! I don't want you!" To say the least, that was not the proper response. In fact, she told people on her job that we were "going together." She also told her husband that I was trying to date her and he called and threatened my life. Later, someone else apparently rejected her. She then told her husband that one of her co-workers had been trying to date her. Her husband went to her job with a gun. When she realized she had endangered that man's life, she admitted she had lied. The people at her place of employment then reasoned that she must have lied about me, too. I learned a valuable lesson. I am more careful now about the way in which I handle an individual's unacceptable idea.

Having considered rejection briefly, let us discuss how it determines the pastor-deacon relationship. In the second chapter, we recognized the fact that the pastor-deacon relationship often starts out negatively due to preconceived notions. These notions create suspicion. Whenever we question people's motives, we treat them differently than someone we trust. We treat them more cautiously. We don't let them get too close; we don't relax with them. They sense the rejection we feel. They observe how we treat others. It is obvious we treat them differently. They feel the rejection. Many respond negatively. They may start vicious rumors. Some start quietly opposing everything suggested by the perceived offender. In time, the opposing party decides the "enemy" has to go. They start working toward that end. If ministers have gained considerable influence with the congregation, attempts to oust them may be futile. But the stage is set for a confrontational, often hostile, relationship.

What is the solution to this dilemma of perceived rejection? All deacons and preachers must value the importance and acceptance of each other as brothers and sisters in Christ. Second, they must realize everyone has feelings and weaknesses. Third, they must appeal to the Bible and the Holy Spirit. Let the Holy Spirit resolve these disputes.

Often, we see "enemies" rather than brothers and sisters in Christ. Christ commands us to love one another (John 13:34). That love constrains our differences. In accepting each other, we understand that rejecting an idea does not equal rejecting a person. Achieving this goal requires constantly reminding each other of God's "agape" love that reigns within our hearts. We let that love show by our treatment of the preacher or the deacons with kindness and forgiveness.

We mistakenly assume that people are cold-hearted. We treat them as we feel they are. This includes negatively talking about them to others and generally snubbing them. Ironically, kindness can win the most cold-hearted person. Regardless of how mean we perceive someone to be, that person can be touched with God's love. If we reaffirm people, we accept them with their strengths and weaknesses. This is a step in the right direction!

The Holy Spirit directly commands us. Therefore, any decision should be in accord with God's Word. When preachers and deacons sense rejection from each other, it becomes an obsession. Many of our deeds are a way of saying, "You will accept me, or else."

THE
QUALIFICATION FACTORS

Let us take a brief look at the term "deacon" and the office of deacon. The term "deacon" occurs in just two passages in the *King James Version* (Phil. 1:1; 1 Tim. 3:8-13), but the Greek word *diakonos*, from which it is taken, appears 30 times. In most cases *diakonos* is translated as "servant" rather than "deacon." In the Greek world, *diakonos* was used to describe the work of a servant. The office of deacon in the New Testament Church may have paralleled the function of a Jewish synagogue assistant, an official who handled the administrative needs of the assembly.

The origin of the office relates to the events of Acts 6:1-6. The Greeks murmured against the Hebrews, alleging discrimination was taking place. Initially, the apostles both preached the Gospel and served the multitudes. This responsibility brought about a heavy workload. When the murmurings began, the apostles consequently called the multitude together and instructed them to choose seven men. They stated the qualifications these men were to possess. They were to be of honest character, full of the Holy Ghost, and wise.

Interestingly, too few of our deacons exhibit signs of being full of the Holy Ghost. Others are not of good report. As a church organizer, I addressed the question of the diaconate in our congregation. Since all churches need deacons (I thought), I hastily selected the deacons. Of the three men who joined the first night, I immediately made two of them deacons, with little concern about their qualifications. One lasted two months, during which time he was arrested and jailed for drunk driving. Behind bars, he made promises about his desire to stop drinking. "I might even preach," he said. Upon release, he came to our worship place as drunk as ever. Within another month, he permanently disappeared.

I did not teach our deacons the proper function of the office. Not until I studied the scriptural directives did our deacons begin to follow the proper guidelines. I wholeheartedly advise any pastor who plans to ordain deacons to train them thoroughly according to biblical directives. Your deacons more likely will be a help and not a hindrance.

When people are chosen for the diaconate, they are introduced to two factions: those who have been on the board for years and those who have rejected the biblical model for their own preferences. These deacons attempt to sway the new deacons before the other side gets to them. Jesus is the divine Head of the Church, and the pastor is the undershepherd. The deacons assist the pastor in the spiritual administration of the church. Sincere deacons who love the Lord know their job. They don't try to take the pastor's job. In such deacons, you have jewels.

At the beginning of this chapter, I gave the biblical qualifications for deacons: men of good report and men of integrity and honesty. Yet a grossly missed qualification is "full of the Holy Ghost." Sadly, many deacons are not willing to discuss the Holy Spirit. Some of their decisions, recommendations, actions, and attitudes cause one to wonder whether they have the Holy Ghost. I have seen men and women on fire for the Lord, full of fervor and energy, cooled by the selection to the deacon board. They mimic judges, welding power and influence.

Paul gave additional qualifications for a deacon in 1 Timothy 3:8-13:

> "Likewise must the deacons be grave, not double-tongued, not given to much wine, not greedy of filthy lucre; Holding the mystery of the faith in a pure conscience. And let these also first be proved; then let them use the office of a deacon, being found blameless. Even so must their wives be grave, not slanderers, sober, faithful in all things. Let the deacons be the husbands of one wife, ruling their children and their own houses well. For they that have used the office of a deacon well purchase to themselves a good degree, and great boldness in the faith which is in Christ Jesus."

These qualifications clearly depict deacons as serious-minded people who speak with honesty and integrity. Likewise, their actions must agree with their principles. Essentially, the new life of a deacon must be accomplished with an equally powerful new lifestyle. Deacons, therefore, should undergo a period of training in order to fulfill the office of deacon.

The spouse of a deacon must also be examined seriously. A deacon's spouse must be sincere and not a gossiper and should be acknowledged for having a mature Christian faith.

"Husband of one wife" is probably the most misunderstood qualification. Some churches argue that if a man has divorced and remarried, he cannot be a deacon because he has "two living wives." This text, however, does not exclude previously married men from the diaconate. But it alludes to the practice of polygamy, when a man has several wives at once. In biblical times, men practiced polygamy openly. Even God-fearing men of the Old Testament practiced polygamy (Caleb, David, Solomon, Asher, etc.). Yet God did not endorse this practice. God endorsed only monogamy, meaning one wife at a time. My argument is not an endorsement of divorce. Divorce, at any time, is unfortunate. Yet one realizes that God does not ordain all marriages. Hence, God does not honor those marriages that are not sanctioned by the Holy Spirit. Who then would be held responsible by God to stay in an ungodly marriage? The church then should more closely evaluate its insistence that previously married men be excluded from the diaconate. Also, the Bible does not teach that a deacon must be married.

Paul is very definite about the deacon's position in the family. Deacons must keep their children in subjection and rule their houses well. Ruling one's house does not mean threats and violence, but love. Love leads a deacon to occupy the role of leadership in the home. The deacon is expected to have an exemplary home life, to be a proven leader, and to possess a flawless character.

Twentieth century deacons hardly resemble the biblical ideal of Holy-Ghost-led people of God. Churches have been subjected to power struggles, faulty leadership, and even ungodly people who have very little regard for God's Word as they attempt to serve as deacons. Many churches have resorted to term limits for deacons to balance this unfortunate occurrence. Term limits prevent one deacon from becoming firmly entrenched in power and impeding the progress of the church. I hope this chapter sufficiently inspires you to study more of the biblical model for deacons.

Because trustees are also officers of the church, a few words should be said about that office. The Bible speaks of two offices in the church: the preacher and the deacon. Later, the office of trustee was added to the church. The organizational structure of the church became more complex as the church grew. Both deacons and trustees were needed to care for the church. Deacons assist with the spiritual affairs of the church. Trustees handle the physical affairs of the church. I expect the same qualifications in a trustee as in a deacon. In many instances, deacons serve simultaneously as trustees. (Trustees mainly manage budgets, building maintenance, loans, fundraising programs, and other projects mandated by the church.) In order to conduct the business of the church, trustees must exemplify the qualifications required of the deacons.

THE PREACHER

Baptists believe that preachers should be divinely called by God. As a consequence, only preachers truly know whether they have indeed been called by God. Some preachers misinterpret a call to preach. God called them, but not to preach.

Too many Baptist preachers assume that the call to preach is simple enough. "You don't have to go to school for preparation. Open your mouth, and God will speak for you." The only preparation some preachers obtain is listening to other preachers. Using a tape and studying the techniques of a preacher they admire, they become carbon copies, focusing on style rather than substance. I do not advise this kind of preparation. The preacher who mimics somebody else can never fully become the preacher God wants the individual to become. God wants us to be unique individuals and not clones. Too many preachers perfect the techniques of celebration. They are talented and gifted enough to have a good "whoop" and touching voices that elicit emotion from the audience. I do not minimize the celebration. When a preacher truly delivers the Word of God, there is nothing more beautiful than the celebrative moment. This style is our heritage; it stirs our souls. If, however, the minister has not used intellect, challenged us to do something, or reminded us to examine our ways, then all of the whooping becomes "junk food." Junk food tastes good but has no real nourishment. An emotional high soon wears off. Christian growth is stunted by poor spiritual nutrition.

Tragically, many preachers worry about "small" things first. They do not get the most important things in proper perspective. Most feel after six months of preaching, they deserve ordination. They become angry if the pastor doesn't hasten to ordain them. If they are not asked to preach the 11 a.m. service, they insist that the pastor is selfish. "He must feel threatened by me." The Sunday morning message is not a time for practicing. There are impressionable souls expecting a word from the Lord. God holds pastors responsible for the parishioners. I have had preachers leave our fellowship, accusing me of not giving them a chance. I had to protect the parishioners from ill-prepared messages.

Let's examine the qualifications of a preacher. Previously mentioned, the divine call is the first criterion. However, I also believe the Bible when it says, "Many are called, but few are truly chosen." God intends for the preacher to enter a state of preparation for ministry. Paul went through three years of preparation before officially presenting himself as an apostle of Jesus Christ. The disciples attended school daily with the Master for three and a half years. He taught them the beautiful truths about the kingdom of God. Likewise, God chooses those persons who are willing to do whatever it takes to become a genuine and faithful minister of Jesus Christ. I am not one who believes you have to have a degree to be effective. But I do believe you need to avail yourself of proper biblical training. If you don't have formal degrees, you may attend a good Bible school or get training in a certificate course. Whatever you do, "Study to show thyself approved unto God, a workman that needeth not to be ashamed, rightly dividing the word of truth" (2 Tim. 2:15). Far too many of God's children have been led astray by false exegesis of the Scriptures by self-taught preachers. I shudder when I think of some of the things I said from the pulpit as a young minister. I earnestly desire for God to blot out the memories of those things. Preachers should examine themselves and ask the question, "To how many people have I given wrong directions?"

Next, preachers should be knowledgeable about the call on their lives. Not everyone was called to pastor; some were called to evangelize or some other work of ministry. The problem arises when preachers become engrossed in their egos. They fall for the illusion that ministry is not genuine unless they are ordained as pastors. Many preachers arrive at this conclusion by listening to the wrong people. Many preachers have announced a call because some people said, "You look like a preacher. You act like a preacher." If you handle Scripture well, they will tell you, "I know you've been called." Preachers who follow such "advice" end up as thoroughly frustrated preachers. People will invariably ask these questions of a preacher: "Where do you pastor? Are you ordained?" If the answers to these questions are negative, they simply walk off. It is as if they say, "Just like I thought, you're a jackleg." No preacher wants to be known as a "jackleg." Because of this fear, they rush to be ordained and called to the pastorate.

When we consider biblical models, evangelists and not pastors did some of the most effective preaching. What about the ordination of evangelists? Early during the twentieth century, it was more difficult to obtain ordination. The early preacher knew the doctrine. The Baptist doctrine said the title "Reverend" was reserved for ordination. Preachers were to be addressed as "Brother" (or "Sister") until ordination. Ordination followed a specific call, such as pastor or assistant pastor, who administered the ordinances of the church. Otherwise, there was no need for ordination. The pastor of a given church may also elect to ordain a minister for some specific work. What is ordination? It confirms a work that God has already begun in a preacher. If God divinely called a minister, the minister need not fret over ordination. Dwight L. Moody was rejected for ordination by his own church. Tradition held that his English and public mannerisms were so atrocious that his own church refused his ordination. Yet he became one of the most effective preachers of his day. Don't worry about being ordained. If God calls and appoints you to a work, ordination will follow naturally.

Why do I stress education? Do I reject someone who has not gone to school? The answer is no. Some of the most fruitful preachers were not formally educated. My father molded my ministry through his example. He didn't have an equal opportunity to attend school, although it burned within his heart. His grandfather was a slave who was not allowed to read. Therefore, he did not fully appreciate education. My father had to work in the field rather than study. As occasion allowed, he enrolled in Bible courses. Those who witnessed his ministry truly attest: "How can a man do these things, except God be with him?" God still uses preachers who have not been formally educated. Education does not define a preacher; it sharpens one's spiritual tools. It empowers one to speak from a position of authority. It gives acceptance in circles that would be closed otherwise, but one must remember that God's calling is more urgent than the need to be an educated member of the Christian family.

I sincerely believe that many denominations exist today because too many teachers, who are not trained in the Word, began movements based upon their own faulty understanding of the Word. After so many years of preaching a faulty doctrine, they refuse to correct their mistakes. Therefore, the pastorate comes with the grave responsibilities of true doctrine. At the dawn of the 21st century, the churches that will survive will be those that demand qualified preachers. Now, let us clarify the qualifications of a pastor. Paul enumerates the qualifications in 1 Tim. 3:2-7:

> "A bishop then must be blameless, the husband of one wife, vigilant, sober, of good behavior, given to hospitality, apt to teach; Not given to wine, no striker, not greedy of filthy lucre; but patient, not a brawler, not covetous; One that ruleth well his own house, having his children in subjection with all gravity; (For if a man know not how to rule his own house, how shall he take care of the church of God?) Not a novice, lest being lifted up with pride he fall into the condemnation of the devil. Moreover he must have a good report of them which are without; lest he fall into reproach and the snare of the devil."

The New Testament uses four terms to describe the leadership of the church:

1. **Elder**—Emphasizes the authority that the leadership has to teach or rule in the church.
2. **Bishop**—Stresses the duty that the leadership has in overseeing the local church and is responsible for the spiritual well-being of the church.
3. **Pastor**—Prioritizes the responsibility to shepherd the flock. Shepherds do not give birth to sheep. The leaders of the church handle for the sheep what they cannot do for themselves. They preserve the good spiritual condition of the sheep and equip them to beget other sheep.
4. **Deacon**—Means to serve. This term illuminates the attitude that one should have in service. Deacons do not govern over the flock. They must realize that they are servants for those the Lord places in their care.

As one carefully examines the scriptural directives of pastoring, the gravity of the job becomes more apparent. Who, knowing the importance of the calling, would dare desire the office without prior qualifications and preparation? Like pilots who have the responsibility of protecting the lives of their passengers, pastors possess the responsibility of securing the souls of all those put under their charge. A few words about the personality of the preacher are appropriate before we conclude this chapter. Pastoral characteristics should include:

(a) vision
(b) great compassion
(c) the fruit of the Spirit and
(d) tenderness toward all people regardless of their differences.

I have not exhausted this discussion on the qualifications. But, should pastors and deacons digest this chapter, a positive change in the pastor-deacon rapport will result.

THE HOLY GHOST
FACTOR

One of the greatest mistakes that pastors and deacons make is the neglect of the Holy Spirit as the Supreme Arbitrator within conflicts. When the Holy Spirit is omitted, tragedy results. This perennial problem in the majority of Baptist Churches reflects a weakness in the teaching ministry. A pastor friend of mine related his experience. While pastoring in Ohio, he taught and preached on the Holy Spirit. One of the deacons met with him after a service and said, "Reverend, we don't want any of that in here." The deacon was so naive about the Holy Spirit. He didn't want to hear about the Holy Spirit. Let's face it, when it comes to teaching about the Holy Spirit, many of us are woefully lacking. The following few pages will detail the workings of the Holy Spirit. I hope the reader will acquire a deeper appreciation for the Holy Spirit. Furthermore, I pray that preachers and deacons will allow the Holy Spirit to resolve the existing, smoldering arguments.

God is a triune being. Three distinct personalities form the Godhead: God the Father, Son, and Holy Spirit. Biblical history, accordingly, divides into three parts. In the beginning, God spoke directly to human beings. When Jesus came, God spoke through

Him. When Jesus returned to heaven, the Holy Spirit began His rule, and now God speaks through the Spirit. The Old Testament prophesied that Jesus would come. God announced His coming through angels who sang of the blessed event, "Glory to God in the highest, and on earth peace, good will toward men" (Luke 2:14). John the Baptist announced that the Savior had arrived, "Repent ye: for the kingdom of heaven is at hand" (Matt. 3:2). When it was time for the Holy Ghost, Jesus announced His coming: "I will not leave you comfortless: I will come to you" (John 14:18). Before His ascension, Jesus promised the Holy Ghost's arrival would be characterized by the apostles receiving power to become witnesses throughout the world.

Although the personalities of the Godhead ruled at specific times, in the beginning they cooperated, "Let us make man." Jesus comforted Shadrach, Meshach, and Abednego when Nebuchadnezzar ordered them thrown into the fiery furnace. When the king looked inside, he saw four and identified the fourth as one "like the Son of God" (Dan. 3:25). The Holy Ghost would empower certain people at various times to complete specific tasks. On the Day of Pentecost, He descended. He is present and works in the lives of those who have accepted Jesus. A lot of confusion exists about the Holy Ghost. Even after this book is published, the confusion will remain. If just one person better understands the function of the Holy Spirit, then this book has been worth the effort.

The Holy Spirit simply means "the Spirit of God." People mystify the Person of the Holy Spirit. Some brag as if they have a monopoly on the Holy Spirit. They have the secret to His special anointing. There are those who appoint themselves as judges to determine whether or not anyone really has the Holy Spirit.

Salvation means that the individual has invited Jesus into his or her heart. Jesus doesn't come alone. He brings God. And God brings the Holy Spirit. It's a package deal. The Three are of one essential element. If I may illustrate, water is an example. In its pure stage, you have water. If heated to boiling, this same water becomes steam. If frozen, it becomes ice. Paul, in the Book of Colossians, affirms that in Christ dwells the fullness of the Godhead bodily. Do you want the Holy Spirit? Invite Him. He will come. Jesus says, "Ask, and it shall be given" (Matt. 7:7; Luke 11:9). How does one receive the Holy Spirit? As one makes room in one's life, the Holy Spirit claims the space until it becomes full. Another illustration using water shows that I cannot replace a glass of water with milk until I empty it out. Likewise in our lives, until we empty ourselves of our sinful ways, we cannot receive the Holy Spirit.

Let us consider some characteristics of the Spirit. The Holy Spirit always is. He retains the same characteristics as the two other Persons in the Godhead. He is omnipresent, omnipotent, and omniscient. Therefore, one does not have to wait until the Holy Spirit comes. He came on the Day of Pentecost. One only has to ask Him to come into his or her heart.

More confusion emerges when some people experience a dramatic indwelling of the Holy Spirit. Confused, they often believe the way the Holy Spirit manifested Himself in their lives is the norm. God does not deal with every person in the same manner. The Bible demonstrates that God deals with each of His servants individually. God made each of us differently. Too many people judge others because they are not emotional. They declare certain congregations spiritually dead. Emotional fervor is not a sign of the Holy Spirit. Emotion arises easily when one is in pain. There are other causes of emotional outbursts than the Holy Spirit.

Jesus gave the first authentic sign of the Spirit's dwelling when He said, "By this all men will know that you are my disciples, if you love one another" (John 13:35, NIV). Additionally, Paul mentions love first as a fruit of the Spirit. He names eight other fruit of the Spirit: joy, peace, long-suffering, gentleness, goodness, faith, meekness, and temperance (Gal. 5:22-23). To truly tell if one has the Holy Spirit, look for the fruit of the Spirit in a believer's life.

What about the gifts of the Spirit? The gifts of the Spirit are the surest evidence of the Holy Spirit in one's life. I reject the notion than everyone must have the gift of tongues as proof of the Holy Spirit. Paul admonishes us to earnestly seek the higher gifts. He says, "Though I speak with the tongues of men and of angels, and have not charity, I am become as sounding brass, or a tinkling cymbal" (1 Cor. 13:1).

The Holy Spirit touches our lives in many ways. He teaches us; He leads us; He calls things back to memory; He convicts us of sin; He is a constant companion, and He can even lift our spirits. He aids in bringing our prayers before God's throne. According to Romans 8, He makes the communication proper as we pray, putting it in a form acceptable to God.

Why did I launch such a discussion of the Holy Spirit? First, I gave the spiritualistic terms for the work of the Holy Spirit. Second, I trust that deacons and preachers everywhere realize there is no need to fight each other. There is no need to take each other to court. This is against the will of God. If we allow the Holy Spirit to control our lives, actions, thoughts, and wills, when conflict arises we can agree as brothers and sisters in Christ if we submit the problem to God. We will find a solution that esteems everybody. Church splits, physical fights, vocal arguments, and court fights occur when preachers, deacons, and congregations refuse to allow the Holy Spirit to rule and reign in their hearts and minds.

Is there a disturbance in your church? What part do you play? Have you allowed the Holy Spirit to govern your actions? You can make a difference! Go to the opposing factions and exhort them to forget their personal grievances. Encourage them to allow the Holy Spirit to become the Supreme Arbitrator.

WHAT ARE WE DOING WRONG?

In any town, there is a church in trouble. More often than not, the controversy involves the preacher and the deacons. Usually, there is a power play. Who is in power? Who runs the church? We realize that it is a spiritual war. There is no effective ongoing communication. Tolerance for the rights of others is nonexistent. God has been left out of the conflict.

Children of God should never forget that the Church remains in a spiritual war against Satan. The devil uses the tactic of divide and conquer against the Church. Confusion is the devil's most reliable strategy. The Bible teaches that God is not the author of confusion (1 Cor. 14:33). When children of God realize we are allowing Satan to use us to foster division in the Church, then we should rely upon the Holy Spirit to mediate our disputes. No reasonable believer should ever think there would never be disagreements in the Church. Some disagreements and strife can be healthy and beneficial as long as the parties differ on issues rather than personalities. Hastily, a lot of preachers and deacons automatically suspect that anyone opposing their ideas dislikes them. This psychological defense mechanism leads to an unfounded paranoia. The merits of the particular issue are lost because the ones who personalize them cannot grasp the real principles because they are busy defending themselves. Satan rejoices over this trouble. Preachers! Deacons! Don't fight each other. Claim Jesus' promise, "Upon this rock I will build my church; and the gates of hell shall not prevail against it" (Matt. 16:18). Recognize that your fight is petty when you consider the magnitude of God.

The power struggle continues when the preacher attempts to assert the full power of the office of pastor. In turn, the deacons hold unswervingly to their right to control of the church. Church people flagrantly disobey the rules of the game. We neglect the directives laid down by the Divine Architect of the Church. It is not surprising that we have problems.

Most power struggles originate with individuals who feel they have been mistreated. If you have anything against a brother or sister in the church, take it to him or her alone. If he or she ignores you, then take two or three witnesses; go again to that sister or brother to substantiate the fact that you followed correct procedures. If that brother or sister refuses to reconcile, take it to the church.

In my experiences of the last 23 years, too many times this has not been properly done. More often than not, those offended go to their closest friends and build a case against the preacher or deacon. In some cases, they discredit their "enemies." This approach curtails the performance of those persons. Such backbiting activity shows a lack of love and a disregard for the teaching of Christ.

Why is the power play so destructive in the church? Several different factors explain this deadly force. Preachers or deacons may feel their personal position or self-esteem is in jeopardy. Unfortunately, there are times when things are fine and those who are guilty fear exposure. There are times when preachers or deacons legitimately feel that they are protecting the church by raising tough issues. In every situation, the church suffers tremendously from unnecessary fighting.

Young people have a saying, "Don't front on me." This means that one of the most painful emotional situations is public embarrassment. When I was growing up, being extraordinarily mischievous, I really didn't mind being punished or reprimanded. Yet if I was spanked in front of my friends, it hurt very deeply. The same thing happens when preachers or deacons feel they have been humiliated publicly. Seldom do preachers or deacons forgive these instances. If either or both have clout in the church, you can see the drawn battle lines. Even if an immediate contest doesn't occur, the newly created "enemy" will wait for another time. When it ripens, the enemy gets revenge. Running battles subject an innocent church to public turmoil and shame.

If there is a fear of corruption, then you can expect the "battle of the ages." Preachers and deacons hold positions of trust. Handling money is a case in point. At the time of the assignment, certain people may be fully trustworthy. Yet if a financial emergency develops and they're holding some church money, they may "borrow" a little to get out of a jam. If another crisis comes, fully intending to put it back, they borrow some more. If disclosure is threatened, their gravy train is threatened, and they may initiate an effort to get rid of the person they hold responsible for the threat.

Another reason conflicts mushroom is bad communication. Jesus' instructions that we go to a brother or sister alone leave the lines of communication open. As long as people communicate, there is a chance at a reasonable resolution. When people stop talking, you can be assured of danger. Effective communication entails more than talk. It also involves listening and sincerely trying to understand the other party's position. Close-minded people want to let others know their intentions, right or wrong.

I have seen preachers and deacons attempt to "massage" each other. They try to get on the good side of the other by publicly making positive statements and giving gifts. But a person with a closed mind has constructed a wall; real communication will not happen. Two parties genuinely interested in a just and equitable solution find it.

Another strange occurrence in church conflict is the willingness to demean, trample, and disregard the rights of others. Such people have emotional problems brought on by past unresolved conflicts. They may have become so bitter they vow never to be hurt again. They seek vengeance against anybody who represents the office of deacon or preacher and who also reminds them of their past unresolved conflict.

I am hardly describing what happens among brothers and sisters who supposedly love the Lord and each other. Little I have said should remind you of the body of Christ. It becomes evident that any pastor or deacon who seeks to serve people should show the evidence of having been filled with the Holy Spirit before assuming a church position. Discarding the qualifications of pastors and deacons increases church problems needlessly. Many church splits can be averted if the opposing factions consult the Holy Spirit with a determination to work purposely toward a solution.

Here is the indictment. Angry church folks have little tolerance for the will of God. When you mention the "real Rulebook," the Bible, they become angrier. I recall a fight between the deacons and pastor that wound up in court. The judge wisely recognized the fact that he could not make a just ruling on the matter. Courts cannot exercise authority in church matters. He ordered the church to get a mediator acceptable to both parties. I was chosen and agreed on by both parties. When I arrived at the meeting, I had a Bible with me, handling it while I talked. One of the deacons asked a question. I started to answer by saying, "The Book says . . ." He cut me off with, "I don't care what the Book says." I replied, "Anyone who doesn't regard what the Book says is a dangerous person." It is tragic that children of God become so angry that they totally disregard God's Word.

To properly fulfill God's plan, the parishioner must see Jesus in the leadership role. If we forget our petty grievances, then preachers and deacons can join hands and fight Satan. As preachers and deacons fight Satan in the name of Jesus, the body of Christ can enjoy eternal peace.

Rules of Order

The lack of trained leadership hampers the effective running of any organization. In this chapter, I offer positive suggestions that can enhance any business meeting. Many arguments can be settled easily by simply observing proper rules. God favors decency and order.

First, let's examine each office and its function. Then we will consider motions. While this will not be an exhaustive discussion, it will encourage the reader to seek additional information in order to become the best preacher or deacon possible.

Chairperson

Generally, the chairperson is the president or moderator in certain circles; the chairperson's duties usually include:

A. Opening the session by calling the members to order. Announcing the business before the assembly. Moving the agenda in order.

B. When necessary, restraining members when engaged in a debate within the rules of order. Enforcing the observance of decorum.

C. Authenticating, by signature, all the acts and proceedings of the assembly. Standing before the assembly, declaring its will, and ensuring obedience to its commands.

D. The chairperson shall put all questions to a vote. The chairperson shall rise when speaking to a question of order. The chairperson shall always use the official title: "The chair decides so and so." When a member has the floor, the chairperson cannot interrupt as long as the person does not transgress the rules of the assembly.

E. The chairperson votes in the occurrence of a vote by ballot. In all other cases, the chairperson votes when his or her vote changes the outcome.

F. The chairperson can appoint a chairperson pro tem; the first adjournment ends that appointment.

If the chairperson wishes to debate, he or she chooses a member to chair the meeting. This should be done rarely. Nothing justifies it in the case of extreme emotion. The chairperson must remain nonpartisan. Otherwise, the ability to control those who are on the opposite side of the question will be lost.

The chairperson must be familiar with parliamentary procedure and set the example of strict conformity to it. The chair shall have executive ability, capable of controlling those served. In order to control others, it is necessary to control one's self. An excited chairperson will certainly cause trouble in a meeting.

The chairperson should not permit the objective of a meeting to be defeated by a few fractious persons using parliamentary procedure with the goal of obstructing business.

The chairperson will become periodically perplexed with the difficulties of the position. Someone once wrote: "The great purpose of all rules and forms is to serve the will of the assembly rather than to restrain it; to facilitate, and not to obstruct, the expression of their deliberate sense."

The Clerk or Secretary

The one responsible for recording the meeting is usually called the clerk or secretary. The record of the proceedings is called the minutes. The secretary should sit near the chairperson. In the absence of the chairperson and vice chairperson, the secretary calls the meeting to order and presides until the election of a chairperson pro tem.

The opening of the minutes should include:

(a) the type of meeting: special or regular,
(b) name of the assembly,
(c) date and place of meeting,
(d) the presence of the chairperson, and in the chairperson's absence the name of the substitutes, and
(e) whether the minutes of the previous meeting were approved.

The minutes should be written in ink in the record book. They should be taken to the meeting and read for approval and corrections. The clerk records the action of the assembly. The clerk should enter each principal motion before the assembly. When there is a division, the clerk enters the number of votes on each side. The clerk should endorse all the reports of committees, the date of their reception, and what further actions were taken upon them. The clerk preserves these reports with the records. The minutes should include a brief summary of each report.

Whereas the minutes and all other official documents remain in the custody of the secretary, they are open for inspection by every member. The chairperson can direct that certain minutes be turned over to a committee that needs them for the proper performance of its duties. The clerk should, prior to each meeting, make out an agenda of business showing in exact order the items to come before the assembly. At each meeting a list of all standing committees and select committees should be available. When a committee is appointed, the clerk should hand the names of the committee and all papers relevant to the chairperson of the committee.

What Is a Quorum?

A quorum of an assembly is the necessary number to transact business. Unless a special rule exists, a quorum of every assembly is a simple majority of all members of the assembly. Whenever an assembly has a permanent existence, the quorum equals less than one-twentieth of its members. This practice becomes a necessity in most large groups, where only a small fraction attends each meeting.

The chairperson should not begin until a quorum is present. If there is no hope of gaining a quorum, then no business can be transacted. The chairperson should adjourn the meeting.

Order of Business

1. Read the minutes of the previous meeting. Seek their approval.
2. Reports of standing committees.
3. Reports of select committees.
4. Unfinished business.
5. New business.

If a special order of the day is approved, it precedes all other business, except the reading of the minutes. If the assembly desires to transact business out of order, it must suspend the rules. Only a two-thirds majority can do this.

Making a Motion

Before a member can offer a motion or address the assembly regarding any matter of business, the member must obtain the floor. The person rises and addresses the presiding officer by title: "Mr.

President" or "Madam President." The chairperson then announces the member's name. When two or more rise at the same time, the chairperson decides who gains the floor by announcing that member's name.

No member who once held the floor is entitled to it again while the same question is before the assembly.

As the interests of the assembly are best served by alternating control of the floor between "pros" and "cons," the chairperson should give preference to a member opposed to the previous speaker. Any member may appeal the decisions of the chairperson. After one offers a motion (someone offers a motion by saying, "I move...") it must be seconded. If not, the motion dies. A motion is not properly seconded until someone obtains the chairperson's attention and then seconds the motion. The chairperson then carries the motion by saying, "It has been properly moved and seconded that..." The chairperson then restates the motion exactly as it was offered. "You have heard the motion; you have had time to consider; are you ready to vote? All in favor, let it be known by saying 'Aye' and those opposing it by saying 'Nay.'" If there are more "Nays" than "Ayes," then the motion dies. If "Ayes" win, then the motion carries, and the action becomes official. When the chairperson asks, "Are you ready to vote?" and someone says, "Not ready," then the chair must recognize those who wish to speak to the issue.

In all my years of meetings, rarely have I seen a meeting that is properly run. Correct meeting procedure eliminates errors and minimizes conflicts.

The Highest Law

In every organization, an absolute and final authority resides. In churches with a hierarchy, the authority rests with the bishop. In the

Roman Catholic Church, the Pope has the ultimate word. In theory, these persons decide matters after they consult with our Lord through the Holy Spirit. In sovereign power churches where the authority rests within the body, it is helpful to address the question of ultimate authority in times of "peace." Rules of order and proper decorum are meaningless if members of the fellowship resist the highest law. This refusal produces conflicts between the deacons and preacher. Too often, each side takes a stand, right or wrong, and refuses to budge. Authority rests in God the Father. God the Son reinforces it. God the Holy Ghost annunciates it. Accordingly, there are some issues that should not be put to a vote. I know a church that split on the issue of worship on the fifth Sunday. The members traditionally attended an Ushers' Convention on the fifth Sunday, and they were not willing to stop. The pastor pushed for a vote. When he lost the vote, the feelings were so polarized that the membership voted him out. Those members who agreed with him left with him and started another church. Sometimes we are our own authority, yet why would anyone have to vote on whether to worship God on the Lord's Day? The error was in voting about something God told us to do thousands of years ago. Another way to have handled the whole matter, allow those who wanted to go to the Ushers' Convention to attend it, and the others who desired to worship on the fifth Sunday to worship.

Now to the question, "What is the highest law?" When Jesus was asked this question, "Which is the greatest commandment?" He responded, "The greatest commandment is the law of love: love for God, self, and neighbors." If we practice this law, it overrides any conflicts. We settle all disputes because we submit to a commandment to love each other. Any issue then becomes secondary to our love for each other. Thereby, we follow God as our Supreme Arbitrator.

So much confusion surrounds love that there is no genuine understanding of how love works. There are different kinds of love. There is "eros," the erotic love between a man and a woman. Next, there is "philos," a brotherly love, a kind of camaraderie between persons in common geography and beliefs. It is a general warmth toward neighbors. The city of Philadelphia takes its name from this kind of love. Hence, it is "the city of brotherly love."

Third, there is "agape." This is the love that God, through Christ, has for us. It is the highest kind of love. It is an unconditional and sacrificial love that we should strive to attain. Sadly, most of our love is conditional. "I will love you as long as you do what I want." In other words, "As long as you please me, I will love you." This is acceptance based on performance. Jesus taught against this type of love. You gain nothing by loving those who love you. Even the "heathens" do that. Instead, Jesus commands us to love "those who spitefully use us." Jesus later says, "By this shall all men know that ye are my disciples, if ye have love one to another" (John 13:35). Paul additionally lists love as the first fruit of the Holy Spirit. If we accept love as the highest law, then it becomes the driving force that mediates conflicts between preachers and deacons.

Having established the highest law, let's apply it to church situations where pastor-deacon conflicts persist. "Because I choose to love, a conscious choice, my love will not allow me to disrespect you. Because you are a child of God, and even though I may thoroughly disagree with you, I will not allow that disagreement to cause me to humiliate you. It will not undermine our love for God." When these dynamics work, resolutions emerge.

Before I conclude this brief chapter on love, I would like to point out the fact that "agape" does not involve an emotion. It involves selflessly seeing and meeting the needs of others less fortunate than yourself. Defining needs confuses many people. For example, I may see a brother who genuinely needs food. I may only have $5, and a meal for him may cost $4.50. I may make a conscious decision to meet his need. Not expecting anything in return or hoping to score extra points with God, I meet the need of someone who needs me. Love and only love motivates us to make conscious decisions to meet needs regardless of the situation. Jesus provides the greatest example of love. Though His enemies were killing Him and even as the sword pierced His flesh, He prayed, "Father, forgive them; for they know not what they do" (Luke 23:34). I pray to perfect this kind of love within me as I seek to better serve the kingdom of God.

Suggestions on How to Resolve a Conflict

1. The moderator, chairperson, president, and pastor should first exhibit love for each person and must demonstrate sensitivity to both sides, even if personally embroiled.

2. Let the group gather first and foremost for prayer and reaffirmation of love for each other-love that will transcend all other issues.

3. Secure a pledge from both sides to settle any conflicts according to biblical principles.

4. Agree to the laws of communication, including effective listening, and not interrupting regardless of how much you disagree.

5. Agree to focus on issues and principles rather than personalities.

6. Constantly reaffirm the presence of the Holy Spirit in the meeting.

7. The litmus test for each issue position is, "Does God approve of the position that I am taking in this conflict?"

8. All people should watch their tone of voice and resist anger. Remember, "A soft answer turneth away wrath: but grievous words stir up anger" (Prov. 15:1).

9. The cause of Christ is bigger than any preacher or deacon board.

10. The moderator ensures that the factions handle themselves in a godly manner.

A
HIDDEN AGENDA

Why do the pastor and certain deacons never agree on anything? Why are they always at odds with each other? The answer lies in the fact that either the preacher or the deacon was offended at some point in the past. Outwardly it seems that all is well, and the incident has been forgotten, but usually the offense has only been repressed. When something is repressed, it is forced into the subconscious mind. The buried offense then influences one's actions, without the person realizing it. One then has misunderstanding, disagreement, and general disgust for the person holding responsibility for the offense but may not realize the reasons for fighting everything the preacher or deacon attempts.

How do we repair a relationship that creates hardship? We must look at the primary cause. It is not necessarily the offense, but it reflects the root of the problem. One of the chief issues of the Bible is forgiveness. No other issue in the Bible is more profound than the need to forgive.

Parenthetically, I must add that the issues of this chapter do not merely apply to preachers and deacons, but to all of God's children. Forgiveness, in God's sight, is not an option. It is a command if we desire God's forgiveness (Matt. 6:14-15). Many members have not been taught the virtue of forgiveness. Consequently, when we have been hurt, we hold the person responsible forever guilty. We withdraw any good feelings for that person. Many say, "If you mess up with me, you'll never have another chance; I'm through with you." However, circumstances force you to interact with the "guilty" party. Not surprisingly, hostilities surface, and one looks for ways to discredit or seek revenge. It becomes a "hidden agenda." I heard a minister say, "I have a trustee who stood up and challenged me when I first started pastoring my church. Since then, whatever he says or tries to do, I chop his head off." Essentially, he was saying, "I have never forgiven him for speaking out against me." That is tragic commentary from a minister of the Gospel. Far too many similar cases exist today, and they fester and grow. Conflicts have a tendency to grow and involve others. Ultimately, the entire church may be included.

What is forgiveness? Can one really forgive and forget? Why does God consider forgiveness so important in the life of the believers? Let's look more closely at the issue of forgiveness.

Forgiveness means that one ceases to hold another responsible for an offense. We occasionally use the saying "forgive and forget." I am sure that we never truly forget; psychologists say that every experience is recorded in the brain. What then is forgiveness? It is remembering without pain. Do you want to know whether you have forgiven someone? When you see the person who mistreated you, if your mood changes and you become angry, then you have not forgiven him or her. God requires that each of us deal with truth in our inward parts (Ps. 51). Until you are willing to put an offense behind you, it will continually haunt you. At the least expected time, it affects the way you handle some situations.

In some pastor-deacon conflicts, the preacher sought peace by publicly praising the deacons. Yet the attempts to win their approval were to no avail. They remained bitter and did everything they could to destroy the preacher. This reveals a fundamental truth: no relationship can move beyond the point of offense until forgiveness becomes a reality. The lack of forgiveness freezes the relationship. Then it degenerates into a worse condition. Compliments given or appeasement will have little effect until the offense has been resolved. Too often, both parties fail to resolve the conflict but determine to prove each other wrong. Then pride prevents the admission of wrongdoing.

How do we resolve such conflicts? Both parties must be willing to admit their mistakes to each other. All too often, ego moves to the forefront. "To admit that I am wrong is the same as bowing to anybody." Parties retreat more deeply into their positions. Accordingly, hostilities grow. Preachers resent certain deacons praying and leading devotion. In turn, the deacons start rejecting the pastor's sermons. God hurts when His children allow conflicts to fester. Ultimately, they destroy the fellowship of a powerful church. This happens because people will not forgive.

Forgiveness is an action of the will and the heart, not the mouth. If one truly desires being right with the Lord, then one wills to do what the Lord commands. What does God command? He commands us to forgive. If we want forgiveness, we must forgive. Why is it so hard to forgive? When a person has been truly hurt, it means that one's selfhood has been attacked; one has been truly humiliated. Degradation strikes at the very existence of one's being. It erodes one's self-esteem. In 22 years of counseling, I have observed that the failure to forgive is invariably linked to the lack of self-forgiveness. Chaos results.

If you have been angry with someone for several years and never have forgiven that person, then God has not forgiven you for your sins. In our prayers we say, "forgive us as we forgive those who trespass against us." In other words, forgive us as we forgive others. Then the Holy Spirit hears, "If I don't forgive others, then don't forgive me." The implications are earth-shattering. Unforgiven sins over a period of years eliminate fellowship with God. No peace within determines one's whole life. Many have acquired psychosomatic illnesses. What affects the mind will eventually affect the body. A person becomes sick without knowing why. Notice the words Jesus used to heal the man who was let down through the roof, "Thy sins be forgiven thee" (Mark 2:5). This suggests that not forgiving others can destroy the fellowship of a church and the one who refuses to forgive.

Should this situation exist in your church or in your personal life, ask the questions, "Is the person I can't forgive worth my relationship with God? Should I destroy the fellowship of many Christians for my selfish reasons?" When we ask these questions, God surely answers, "It's not worth it." How do you begin to forgive? I suggest these steps:

(a) pray for the will to forgive,
(b) find a counselor and discuss your problem,
(c) visualize your healing from the offense, and
(d) act as if God has already healed you. You are well on your way to being healed.

The deacon and the preacher are the only scriptural offices of the church. These divine appointments include the serious responsibility of being exemplary Christians living for others to see. Additionally, Jesus commands us to "love one another." When we follow these directives, our church, official board, and pastor will flourish in God's service.

"I Don't Like Preachers!"

You wouldn't expect people to dislike a person called to preach the Gospel and shepherd souls. Throughout the Bible, preachers who were true to their divine calling were hated and treated cruelly by those they were sent to help. Jeremiah was disgraced before his fellow citizens in the city square (Jer. 26:8-9). John the Baptist was beheaded (Matt. 14:3-12). All of the disciples, with the exception of John, were martyred. Anabaptists were flogged, drowned, and burned at the stake during the Protestant uprising of the 1500s. Countless ministers have been killed and viciously persecuted. One of the most maligned persons in the Christian community is the preacher.

Little myths, like "all preachers love chicken," stereotype the minister. All kinds of jokes, clean and dirty, abound. Everybody knows a preacher joke. The "grapevine" constantly searches for the dirt on prominent preachers. The public closely scrutinizes ministers. Tragically, the world focuses on a few preachers who are known to be dishonest, and all preachers are judged based on the actions of these few. Such generalizations are almost totally inaccurate. Fortunately, we still have countless, excellent preachers who love the Lord. They do an exceptional job in the service of the Lord and the Church.

All this negative talk about "crooked" preachers gives the world a less than rosy view of them as a whole. When preachers are called to a church, they arrive as suspected people. Unfortunately, those who are charged to be their spiritual assistants, the deacons, unify themselves against preachers. A percentage of board members become "preacher haters." These deacons often feel it is their duty to watch preachers so "they don't come in here and change anything." Regrettably, all programs and suggestions advanced by the minister are viewed with suspicion. Given such close scrutiny, they are rendered almost totally ineffective. In frustration, preachers attempt to change things in their favor. A hostile relationship ensues. The success or failure of the ministers' actions depends on the influence gained for their office.

What happens when a hostile relationship exists? Those who love the pastor, usually along with those who recently joined the church, become the pastor's chief advocates. They become polarized with longstanding members. In my experience, I have seen this happen many times. It is simply a dangerous situation. Those who oppose the pastor seek to trick, find something damaging to the pastor's reputation, or discredit the pastor's ministry. The scenario has a formula. A vicious rumor spreads and stirs up the church. Then church members vote the pastor out. A problem arises when it does not work that easily. Occasionally, both sides end up in court. The court usually fails to satisfy both sides. If the minister wins the dispute, the minister may go to the church and find a padlock on the door. Some controversies have escalated to the point of members shooting or injuring other members. Eventually, churches split. The minister leaves with a number of people, and they start a church. I know a church that has given birth to three new churches in 20 years. Needless to say, this excessive fighting has scarred the remaining members.

What can be done? Certainly, there is a way to improve the relationship between preachers and deacons. Officers who fear a loss of influence and power can minimize controversy by:

(a) remaining open-minded,
(b) being willing to reconcile with the minister,
(c) recognizing their proper roles in the church,
(d) allowing the Holy Spirit to take the lead, and (e) following the wishes of the congregation at large.

All ministers, led by the Holy Spirit, have more control over hostile situations than they realize. (See "The Holy Ghost Factor.") With God's approval, preachers can survive insurmountable odds. Ministers should realize when they first arrive, they are not the pastor yet. They must convince the new congregation they truly love them, and this takes time. They must cry with them, bury their dead, visit their sick, and show them a genuine love and concern. It takes three to five years for ministers to become pastors. Demonstrating love does not automatically make them pastors. They must forsake favoritism toward any group in the church. To be sure, when pastors are called, the opposing groups try to win them to their side. Wise ministers will remain neutral. They let the Bible settle the conflicts that emerge. The Holy Spirit leads ministers in such endeavors. A certain minister was called to a known church with the reputation for getting rid of preachers. However, the preacher stayed for years. When asked the question, "How could you stay at that church all these years?" he replied, "I just love the hell out of them." Love wins more wars in the kingdom of God than any court case, underhanded tactic, or deceitful strategy.

Next, preachers must be careful to resist fighting their battles from the pulpit. They should not tailor their sermons to defeat their opponents. Such messages only infuriate them. They will only retreat and utilize more underground tactics. Once, I preached a revival at a church in a distant city, where a young minister had the backing of his church, but his official board solidly opposed him. Because he knew he had the support of the majority, he got up each night and threw stones at his deacons. I recognized this mistake and asked if I could offer some advice. He accepted the advice with thanks but apparently had done irreversible damage. The deacons contacted a minister who didn't like their pastor and trumped up some charges. Although he prevailed in court, he could have prevented unnecessary negative publicity and financial burden by not fighting this battle from the pulpit. The best position preachers can fight from is on their knees!

Many times, deacons fail to recognize that God holds them responsible for peace in the church. They are just as responsible as the minister. When given power and control, people typically hate to give it up. Anything or anyone who threatens our position of power prompts a fight. The fear of the loss of power causes leaders to become hostile. Deacons must view their office from a different perspective. If deacons see their position as a blessed opportunity to serve God, then they want only to please Him. They then regard their position as a service position and not their own power seat. Then, points of contention lose significance.

It is useless to try and convince a close-minded person to look at something differently. I have known many close-minded people. When one is close-minded, nothing goes in and nothing comes out. Many times, this happens with a deacon board. A deacon solidifies a position and refuses to budge at any cost. Close-minded people even ignore the leading of the Holy Spirit. Deacons should remain open to the Lord in decision making. The only way to prevent bitterness between preachers and deacons is to foster willingness on both sides.

How Does a Church
Call a Pastor?

Knowledge about how to call a pastor is scant, at best. Many churches have been surprised by the sudden loss of a pastor. In churches with a hierarchy, the bishop fills pastoral vacancies without the input of the congregation. These congregations belong to the Methodist Church, Church of God in Christ, Episcopal Church, and Roman Catholic Church. Churches that elect their own pastors are usually Baptist, Congregationalist, Presbyterian, and independent churches.

In the Baptist faith, power lies in the congregation. This form of organization allows a local congregation the freedom to determine what it considers the will of God. Thus, each congregation governs its own affairs. Congregational freedom does not imply that the local bodies are self-governing apart from the Lordship of Christ, but the members of each congregation have the right to determine what they consider to be God's will. Pastoral vacancies have led to inappropriate and unjust occurrences in the name of calling a pastor. In the past, the average church member knew the doctrine of the church, but within the past 20 years, less emphasis has been placed on doctrine and discipline within Baptist churches. Ignorance creates many abuses. The following information is basically Baptist in perspective. However, it may help in other situations.

The Baptist church is a democratically run entity, which means that it is ruled by the pleasure of the majority. The Baptist church is a theocratically operated church. This means that God governs. The Bible is the guidebook of instruction, as well as inspiration. When a church becomes vacant, a pulpit committee is elected. The pulpit committee should include a variety of people representative of the congregation. The desired qualifications of the prospective pastor should be determined before the search officially commences. The committee should meet and define the guidelines with input from the church. These guidelines should be presented to the official board for approval. In turn, the official board recommends them to the congregation. The congregation has the final decision on its expectations of a pastor. Many times, while the search for a pastor proceeds, an interim pastor is elected. The interim pastor ensures that pulpit duties, as well as other pastoral duties, are handled while the search for a permanent pastor continues. The interim pastor may or may not be a candidate. However, in most cases, the interim pastor should be a church member or retired minister whose interest in pastoring the church is little or nonexistent. When interim pastors have a deep interest in the church, they may behave in a manner less than proper when other candidates visit.

The pulpit committee should receive recommendations on ministers and résumés, eliminating those who do not meet the qualifications specified. Those ministers who qualify should be contacted and given an opportunity to preach. Often, the pulpit committee does a preliminary investigation that entails looking at how candidates are accepted in their present assignments, the experience the candidates have in pastoring, and looking at their potential for the future. It should not be apparent to the present congregation of a minister that you are interviewing its pastor. Difficulties arise when a congregation discovers that its pastor is seeking another church. Some pastors have been dismissed even though they were not selected for a new pastorate. Favorably, a visit is made to a minister's current congregation without the minister or the congregation knowing.

In the event of an incumbent pastor's death, a period of mourning is generally observed before the search for a new pastor begins. The congregation should agree on this period of time.

When a congregation dismisses a pastor, usually there are open wounds. Rarely is there an overwhelming vote against the minister. This means that those who were in favor of the pastor have to be considered. If the wounded crowd is deeply disturbed, they will become bitter toward those they blame for the disturbance. Many church splits have resulted from such an experience. In cases where both sides remain in the congregation, a hostile tone develops. The hostile faction fights anyone recommended for pastor because the opposing side recommends that person. Such situations require deep prayer and concerted efforts toward reconciliation. The healing of the Holy Spirit brings a "peace that passeth human understanding."

A church should not wait too long to call a minister. A firmly entrenched official board becomes more powerful, and board members are more reluctant to give up their power when a new minister is chosen. They view the new minister as a "hired hand" and may be quick to bring charges against the new minister. Periodically, good pastors have been unfairly dismissed because a powerful board abuses its legitimate authority.

Actually, what authority does the official board have in the church? The official board is not a policy- or decision-making body. Usually, the pastor offers recommendations to the official board. The board, then, considers the matters and, in turn, makes recommendations to the church, which votes on them. Matters raised by the board members should be given full attention in the board meeting. In cases where there is no pastor, the chair of the board presides and presents recommendations.

Now the pulpit committee has a list of candidates. It should seek to be impartial. The committee will interview the candidates to ascertain whether their views on local church administration are generally in line with the perceived direction of the congregation. All candidates should be asked the same basic questions and given an ample opportunity to explain their views. After having heard all the finalists, the pulpit committee should deliberate. They should recommend one candidate to the church. Having multiple candidates can be dangerous and have the potential of further fragmenting the congregation because each candidate will enjoy some support. If the climate is volatile, it may be wise to have a disinterested president chairing the meeting where the call is to be held.

Precautions should be taken to ensure a "call" is conducted fairly. The chair of the meeting should plea for unity when the new pastor is selected. If the church belongs to an association, then the moderator is one preferred leader of the meeting.

The pulpit committee and official board should let the members of the congregation know each step they take during the search process. It is when the congregation is not fully informed that trouble inevitably starts. Many times, the board or pulpit committee is out of touch with the consensus of the congregation. The congregation does not have to accept any candidate for pastor. I know of a case where the pulpit committee did not consider a certain minister. In the call meeting, a member offered his name from the floor. He received more votes than the person recommended by the committee.

It saddens me to think of the many abuses that occur during the call process. When those in charge are more concerned with their own positions and power, abuse is inevitable. Ministers have reportedly made secret deals with dishonest deacons who abuse the process for monetary gains. In such cases, the deacons feel they have something to hold over the minister's head. In this scenario, pastors must agree with the board members against their own judgment.

When the congregation is not aware of its rights, often the ultimate decision is made in the board meeting. Deacons design the way the recommendation is to be presented to the church; then they present it in a manner to assure its success. I have known cases where the congregation favored a certain candidate. Mysteriously, rumors surfaced about this minister and negated the minister's candidacy.

Those of us in leadership positions must understand that the Church does not belong to us. It belongs to Jesus. We must seek the guidance of the Holy Spirit in our decisions, especially when we choose our earthly shepherd to teach us how to have a right relationship with God. We will have to give an account of how we managed the Lord's business.

This chapter suggests the way a church should elect a pastor. It is not my intention to propose it as the only way. A praying church gives the Holy Spirit the lead in all matters, and is, thus, a victorious church.

How Much Do We Pay this Preacher?

Seemingly, nothing is more controversial than the preacher's compensation package. There are those who feel the preachers should work for very little. There are those who are not fond of preachers; they will do anything to keep them from getting a decent salary. There are still others who are not well paid, and they don't want "Reverend" to make more than they do. Often ministers must obtain part-time employment. In some cases, they have had to supplement their income in order to meet their financial obligations, while their congregations pay them the least amount possible. Many times, the congregation votes on elaborate programs for the physical structure with little sympathy for the minister.

Current congregations negotiate salaries with ministers and provide them with a benefits package. Ministers today who invest themselves in congregations are often catalysts for new incoming members. Model churches usually provide:

A. A salary based upon the "church market"
B. A parsonage and living expenses or a housing allowance
C. An automobile
D. Expenses for conventions, meetings, and continuing education

E. Insurance—health and life insurance, a retirement plan, and other benefits

Model churches have a full-time pastor and a vision. Such churches attract ministers of an exceptionally high caliber. I am well aware of churches that struggle to survive. Churches should insure they do all they can for the one they elect to nourish and inspire their souls.

Sometimes ministers die while in service to particular congregations. If their families are in the parsonage, they are sometimes unfairly treated by the congregation. I have heard of a widow and her children being given 30 days to vacate the parsonage. Congregations should be careful not to abuse a deceased pastor's family. After all, the family sacrificed quality time so members of the church could be served.

Furthermore, consideration should be given to furnishing an adequate retirement plan for the minister. Many preachers realize when they have exhausted their fruitfulness at a church. They recognize the signs of negative attendance, declining finances, and the lack of spiritual growth. They even know that many in the congregation want a different or younger minister. People sometimes wonder why the minister just will not leave. It's not that simple. I have seen ministers give their best years to congregations that just want to kick them out. Without a retirement package, giving up the church that pays a salary is hard to do. Congregations could spare themselves a lot of pain and possible courtroom battles by providing a generous retirement program. It could entice a tired minister to retire comfortably and allow the church to move in a new direction. I believe when a church contributes cheerfully and provides for the pastor's welfare, the congregation receives blessings untold, spiritually and financially.

Preachers Called to a Messy Situation—What to Do, What Not to Do

Occasionally, ministers are called to congregations that require special understanding. The new pastor must be an agent of healing to that particular congregation. If a church has split, a long-time pastor has died, or there was a crisis, then prayer, the guidance of the Holy Spirit, and an extra anointing of patience are necessary to begin a corporate healing.

Corporate pain resembles individual pain. When a group is hurting, all feel the commonality of the pain. As a corporate body, they have undergone the same painful experience. If the pain involved another minister, the new preacher starts at a disadvantage when entering the congregation.

Ministers cannot assume they are actually pastors because they have been called to a congregation. Before a congregation will allow you to become the pastor, you have to earn the position. While one may be pastor in name, officially recognized as the pastor, one only becomes the real pastor when one shows many acts of love, marries the young, buries the dead, goes beyond the official call of duty, goes beyond the job description, and shows genuine camaraderie with the community. Ministers only have as much power with congregations as their influence brings them. Their influence depends on their ability to identify the needs of a certain congregation and address those needs in a positive manner.

If churches have split, wise pastors will not enter the conflicts under the belief they are the world's greatest judges. Church members are not yet ready to be told they were wrong. They do, however, want you to affirm they were right in their actions. New pastors are at a disadvantage because they are expected to "fix it all" within the first year. It does not matter to most congregants that they are totally unaware of what happened before their arrival. The members will ensure the new minister is told, in detail, everything that happened. Conventional wisdom suggests that you "don't get too friendly with the crowd that is left or with those who stayed with the home church." New pastors must understand that some members who remained are sympathetic with the other side. Some might have taken a different stance if another family member would have stood with him or her. You risk alienating such a person if you try to reinforce the fact that the "new" church was right all the time.

There is also a faction within the congregation that will visit the other side to watch what is going on with them. They will keep a relationship with someone on the other side and convey all the gossip they hear. If new ministers are wise, they will lovingly let it be known they are not interested in the argument. They do not intend to become participants in situations not involving them. The minister's position is, "I am commanded to love everybody by Jesus. I am here to heal." In other words, the new pastor becomes an agent of peace rather than one who perpetuates strife. In cases where a long-time pastor has died and was loved by the congregation, they will idealize the deceased's memory. In some cases, they will deify the former pastor. Every action the new minister takes will be measured against the deeds of the deceased pastor. The new pastor will hear, "Reverend So and So used to..." New pastors may become jealous of the former pastor and start fighting that memory. If new pastors do this, they are insecure.

New pastors must know they gain nothing by attacking a fond memory. They should actually support the legacy of the former pastor. The new pastor could help the deceased pastor's family financially. In addition, the new pastor should generally show a genuine respect for the memory of the deceased's family. As a result, the congregation would more quickly embrace the new pastor.

Where the congregation is divided, there will be very delicate issues and the need to mend fences. The new minister needs spiritual discernment to recognize areas of pain. The minister should gently lead the congregation to a new level in healing. If the minister leans on the Holy Spirit to guide this ministry, healing will result naturally. Yet the healing process is slow. As one chops down a tree, the first lick with an ax only yields a small chip. But if he or she keeps hitting the same place, the whole tree eventually falls.

In cases where the church lacks organization, the new minister must set up an organization around the people who control most of the power. These people typically enjoy the loose organization. It helps to perpetuate their hold on power. Clear organization means greater accountability. Where there is little accountability, abuses prevail. Large amounts of money are not accounted for. Organizational excellence reveals the underhanded tactics of those who selfishly perpetuate the status quo.

If the minister succeeds in establishing a more accountable organization, the power brokers, who feel the pastor mistreats them, go underground. They quietly fight the minister's program, say a negative word when they can, and present the minister in a negative light. The minister should remain prayerful and be wise as a serpent and harmless as a dove, while giving out large doses of love for every dose of evil thrown at the ministry. In the end, love will be victorious. The defining Scripture is 1 Cor. 15:58, "Therefore, my beloved brethren, be ye steadfast, unmovable, always abounding in the work of the Lord, forasmuch as ye know that your labor is not in vain in the Lord."

It takes extraordinary patience and courage to be an agent of healing. Yet the Lord enables the minister to equip the congregation to carry out the mission that the Lord assigns them.

WHY IS IT THAT BLACK MEN AS A WHOLE DON'T ATTEND CHURCH?

In any black church in the country, you find that the women out-number men disproportionately. Why? Why is it so hard to get black men to participate in the service of the Lord? Many dynam-ics negatively impact the black male. These circumstances subtly discourage him from becoming an ardent supporter of organized religion. In order to understand the refusal of black men to attend church, we must appreciate the black male psyche. It explains the mystery.

Our culture generally discourages the black man's free expres-sion. Subsequently, it inhibits him from fully expressing his faith. However, the same society definitely encourages the black female to express her innermost feelings. When the black girl is young, she is told, "Little girls are made of sugar and spice and everything nice." But boys are made of snails and puppy dog tails. And a man is not supposed to cry. The little girl cries and is encouraged to tell Mama what's wrong. The little boy cries and is told, "You can han-dle your own problems." When he grows up, he is told to go to church. "The preacher can help you with your problems." Yet he remembers his childhood lesson, "You can handle your own problems." He then refuses to allow anybody to tell him the things he has had to handle.

Also, many black males will not go to church out of jealousy. They hear their wives speak admiringly of the minister. Because his mate talks about "Reverend" so much, he unconsciously builds up a resistance. He sees the preacher as competition; the man misinterprets his mate's admiration to mean that she is "in love" with the minister. He resents the church and the pastor. In many cases, he hassles his mate about "staying at church all of the time." He never passes up the opportunity to berate the church and the preacher.

Many reasons abound. An overwhelming number of black men are underemployed. This increases the chances that they will be talked down to by their supervisors. At home, their mates do the same. As a consequence, they will not willingly go to church and have the minister talk down to them, too. I would encourage ministers to examine how they present their messages to the men of the congregation. Our 8:00 A.M. Sunday service has as many men as women. It is inspirational to see several hundred black men at that service. I ensure that the male is well respected. I highlight male accomplishments. I do not favor the ladies against the men in the messages that I preach. Black men appreciate affirmation.

Many ministers and deacons have not been wise. They are very obvious in flirting with another man's wife. I hate to admit it, but our record as Christian leaders needs improvement. Many of us should bow at the cross with full repentance because of the difficulties we have caused in the homes of others. Many men refuse to go to church because a church leader took their mate. As these disillusioned men share their tragic stories, the word gets around, "Don't trust church folk."

I strongly encourage us as ministers to consider our actions as we evangelize the black male. Let's not be too friendly with their mates. Let's stop making remarks that can be taken out of context. If we will ever rebuild their trust, we must try harder to be more concerned about the salvation of the Christian family than our own personal gratification.

There is another factor that affects the black male's church attendance. It deals with the way the man perceives himself. If he lacks confidence in his abilities, he would rather skip church. He may be afraid to be singled out in church. I cannot possibly exhaust the reasons why the black male has abandoned the church. But I do believe we can reclaim him.

Addendum

CHURCH COVENANT

Having been led by the Spirit of God to receive the Lord Jesus Christ as our Savior, and on the profession of our faith, having been baptized in the name of the Father, and of the Son, and of the Holy Spirit, we do now in the presence of God, angels, and this assembly most solemnly and joyfully enter into covenant with one another, as one body in Christ.

We engage, therefore, by the aid of the Holy Spirit, to walk together in Christian love; to strive for the advancement of this church in knowledge and holiness; to give it a place in our affections, prayers, and services above every organization of human origin; to sustain its worship, ordinances, discipline, and doctrine; to contribute cheerfully and regularly, as God has prospered us, toward its expenses, for the support of a faithful and evangelical ministry among us, the relief of the poor, and the spread of the Gospel throughout the world. In case of difference of opinion in the church, we will strive to avoid a contentious spirit, and if we cannot unanimously agree, we will cheerfully recognize the right of the majority to govern.

We also engage to maintain family and secret devotion; to study diligently the Word of God; to religiously educate our children; to seek the salvation of our kindred and acquaintances; to walk circumspectly in the world; to be kind and just to those in our employ and faithful in the service we promise others, endeavoring in purity of heart and good will toward all men to exemplify and commend our holy faith.

We further engage to watch over, to pray for, to exhort, and to stir up each other unto every good word and work; to guard each other's reputation, not needlessly exposing the infirmities of others; to participate in each other's joys and, with tender sympathy, bear one another's burdens and sorrows; to cultivate Christian courtesy; to be slow to give or take offense but always ready for reconciliation, being mindful of the rules of the Savior in the 18th chapter of Matthew, to secure it without delay; and through life, amid evil report and good report, to seek to live to the glory of God, who hath called us out of darkness into His marvelous light.

When we move from this place, we engage as soon as possible to unite with some other church in fellowship where we can carry out the spirit of this covenant and the principles of God's Word.

ARTICLES OF FAITH

The Articles of Faith, which should be adopted by Baptist churches at the time of organization:

I. The Scriptures

We believe the Holy Bible was written by men divinely inspired and is a perfect treasure of heavenly instruction, and it has God for its author, salvation for its end, and truth without any mixture of error for its matter; that it reveals the principles by which God will judge us and, therefore, is, and shall remain to the end of the world, the center of Christian union and the standard by which all human conduct, creeds, and opinions shall be tried.

II. The True God

We believe the Scriptures teach that there is one, and only one, living and true God, an infinite, intelligent Spirit, whose name is Jehovah, the Maker and Supreme Ruler of heaven and earth; inexpressibly glorious in holiness and worthy of all possible honor, confidence, and love; that in the unity of the Godhead there are three People-the Father, the Son, and the Holy Ghost-equal in every divine perfection and executing distinct but harmonious offices in the great work of redemption.

III. The Fall of Man

We believe the Scriptures teach that man was created in holiness, under the law of his Maker, but by voluntary transgression, fell from the holy and happy state; in consequence of which all human beings are sinners, not by constraint but by choice; being the nature utterly void of that holiness required by the law of God, positively inclined to evil, and, therefore, under just condemnation to eternal ruin, without defense or excuse.

IV. The Way of Salvation

We believe the Scriptures teach that the salvation of sinners is wholly of grace through the mediatorial office of the Son of God, who by the appointment of the Father, freely took upon Him our nature, yet without sin, honored the divine Law by His personal obedience, and by His death made a full atonement for our sins; that having risen from the dead, He is now enthroned in heaven; and uniting in His wonderful person the tenderest sympathies with divine perfections, He is in every way qualified to be a suitable, compassionate, and all-sufficient Savior.

V. Justification

We believe the Scriptures teach that the great Gospel blessing, which Christ secures to those who believe in Him, is justification; that justification includes the pardon of sin and the promise of eternal life on principles of righteousness; that it is bestowed, not in consideration of any works of righteousness we have done, but solely through faith in the Redeemer's blood; by virtue of which faith His perfect righteousness is freely imputed to us of God; that it brings us into a state of most blessed peace and favor with God and secures every other blessing needful for time and eternity.

VI. The Freeness of Salvation

We believe the Scriptures teach that the blessings of salvation are made free to all by the Gospel; that it is the immediate duty of all to accept them by cordial, penitent, and obedient faith; and that nothing prevents the salvation of the greatest sinner on earth but his or her own determined depravity and voluntary rejection of the Gospel, and that such rejection involves him or her in an aggravated condemnation.

VII. Regeneration

We believe the Scriptures teach that in order to be saved, sinners must be regenerated, or born again; that regeneration consists in giving a holy disposition to the mind and heart that it is affected in a manner above our comprehension by the power of the Holy Spirit in connection with divine truth to secure our voluntary obedience to the Gospel; and that its proper evidence appears in the holy fruits of repentance, faith, and newness of a life in obedience to Christ.

VIII. Repentance and Faith

We believe the Scriptures teach that repentance and faith are sacred duties and also inseparable graces, wrought in our souls by the regenerating Spirit of God; whereby being deeply convinced of our guilt, danger, and helplessness and of the way of salvation by Christ, we turn to God with unfeigned contrition, confession, and supplication for mercy, at the same time heartily receiving the Lord Jesus Christ as our Prophet, Priest, and King and relying on Him alone as the only and all-sufficient Savior.

IX. God's Purpose of Grace

We believe the Scriptures teach that the election is the eternal purpose of God, according to which He graciously regenerates, sanctifies, and saves sinners; that being perfectly consistent with the free agency of man, it comprehends all the means in connection with the end; that is a most glorious display of God's sovereign goodness, being infinitely free, wise, holy, and unchangeable; that it utterly excludes boasting and promotes humility, love, prayer, praise, trust in God, and active imitation of His free mercy; that it encourages the use of means in the highest degree; that it may be ascertained by its effects in all who truly believe the Gospel; that it is the foundation of Christian assurance and that to ascertain it with regard to ourselves demands and deserves the utmost diligence.

X. Sanctification

We believe the Scriptures teach that sanctification is the process by which, according to the will of God, we are made partakers of His holiness; that it is a progressive work; that it is begun in regeneration, and that it is carried on in the hearts of believers by the presence and power of the Holy Spirit, the Healer and Comforter, in the continual use of the appointed means, especially the Word of God, self-examination, self-denial, watchfulness, and prayer.

XI. Perseverance of Saints

We believe the Scriptures teach that such only are real believers as endure to the end; that their persevering attachment to Christ is the grand mark which distinguishes them from superficial professors; that a special Providence watches over their welfare, and they are kept by the power of God through faith unto salvation.

XII. The Law and Gospel

We believe the Scriptures teach that the Law of God is the eternal and unchangeable rule of His moral government; that it is holy, just, and good, and that the inability of fallen men to fulfill the Scripture's precepts arises entirely from fallen man's love of sin; that one great end of the Gospel is to deliver fallen men from this sin and to restore them to unfeigned obedience to the holy Law through a Mediator and through the means of grace connected with the establishment of the visible church.

XIII. A Gospel Church

We believe the Scriptures teach that a visible church of Christ is a congregation of baptized believers associated by covenant in the faith and fellowship of the Gospel, observing the ordinances of Christ, governed by His laws, and exercising the gifts, rights, and privileges invested in them by His Word; that its only scriptural officers are bishops or pastors and deacons whose qualifications, claims, and duties are defined in the epistles of Timothy and Titus.

XIV. Baptism and the Lord's Supper

We believe the Scriptures teach that Christian baptism is the immersion in water of a believer into the name of the Father, and Son, and Holy Ghost; to show forth in a solemn and beautiful emblem our faith in the crucified, buried, and risen Savior, with its effect in our death to sin and resurrection to a new life; that it is pre-requisite to the privileges of a church relation and to the Lord's Supper, in which the members of the church, by the sacred use of bread and wine, are to commemorate together the dying love of Christ, preceded always by solemn self-examination.

XV. The Christian Sabbath

We believe the Scriptures teach that the first day of the week is the Lord's Day, or Christian Sabbath, and is to be kept sacred to religious purposes by abstaining from all secular labor and sin-ful recreations, by the devout observance of all the means of grace, both private and public, and by preparation for the rest that remaineth for the people of God.

XVI. Civil Government

We believe the Scriptures teach that civil government is of divine appointment for the interest and good order of human society; and that magistrates are to be prayed for, conscientiously honored, and obeyed, except only in things opposed to the will of our Lord Jesus Christ who is the only Lord of the conscience.

XVII. Righteous and Wicked

We believe the Scriptures teach that there is a radical and essential difference between the righteous and the wicked; that only through faith are those justified in the name of the Lord Jesus, sanctified by the Spirit of our God, and truly righteous in His esteem; while all others who continue in impenitence and unbelief are in His sight wicked and under the curse; and this distinction holds among men both in and after death.

XVIII. The World to Come

We believe the Scriptures teach that the end of the world is approaching; that at the last day, Christ will descend from heaven and raise the dead from the grave for final retribution; that a solemn separation will then take place; that the wicked will be judged to endless punishment and the righteous to endless joy; and that this judgment will fix forever the final state of human beings in heaven or hell on principles of righteousness.

NOTES

Printed in the United States
63593LVS00002B/1-357